END TIMES
BOOK

THE
RAPTURE
THE MARK OF THE
BEAST
THE
ANTICHRIST
AND MORE
REVISITED!

W. E. SMITH

Copyright © 2024 W.E. SMITH

All rights withheld. Without the prior written permission of the author, no part of this publication may be reproduced, circulated, or transmitted in any form or through any means, including photocopying, recording, or other electronic or mechanical methods, except for brief quotations embodied in critical reviews and some other non-commercial uses allowed under copyright law.

Author: W.E. SMITH
Project manager W.E. SMITH
WillHouse Publishing LLC
Website: books2read.com/willhousepublishing

This book may be purchased for educational, business, or promotional purposes. For information, kindly contact the publisher by email. To contact this Author for Speaking Engagements, Book Signings, Questions, or to be added to a mailing list for events and upcoming book releases please email us at.

WillHousePublishing@gmail.com

Quotes from:
Unless otherwise noted, Scripture quotations are from the King James Version (KJV), 1604, or The American Standard Version (ASV), officially Revised Version, Standard American Edition, 1901

Book Cover Art:
Licensed from Freepik.com for Unlimited Use without Attribution

Other Books by this Author:

"My Time with the Devil"
And The Truth about Hell, Satan & Spiritual Warfare
By W. E. Smith

I was a victim of demonic attacks often. I was physically beaten and haunted by evil spirits for many years. Then it all stopped. In this book, I will tell my True Story of demonic abuse, how I've been free from it for over a decade, and how you can be free as well. We will Uncover the Truths about Lucifer, Eternal Damnation, the power of Death, the Biblical names of Satan, and the Essence of Evil.

Audiobooks, ebooks, & paperbacks, @
http://books2read.com/WillHousePublishing

"Healing Rainbows"
Embracing the LGBTQ with Scriptures
By W. E. Smith

"Healing Rainbows" Exposes every Biblical Myth & Misunderstood Scripture used to condemn the Gay Community. This is NOT a book promoting Gay or Trans rights, etc. The Author is a Straight Christian Man who used to use scriptures to attack the Gay community, but after much study, he realized he was wrong. If you are a member of the LGBT community & concerned that you are going to Hell, or If you are a Parent torn between Accepting your LGBT Child or Obeying God & His Word, then this book, "Healing Rainbows," is for you. This book uses the Holy Scriptures to prove its points. God is Love & loves EVERY community, and His Son Jesus even confirms them in scripture. "Healing Rainbows" will show you! It is a book about Love, Truth, Understanding, and Healing.

Audiobooks, ebooks, & paperbacks, @
http://books2read.com/WillHousePublishing

"End Nail Biting Forever!"
By W. E. Smith

Within this little book's pages is a simple yet phenomenally effective solution showing you how to STOP biting your nails Forever. There are no gimmicks, tricks, creams, or chemicals, just a proven way to end the horrible nail-biting habit. These are simple everyday actions that will immediately change your nail-biting behavior. This book is short, sweet, and to the point. You Can STOP Today!

For ebooks or paperbacks, go to
http://books2read.com/WillHousePublishing

TABLE OF CONTENTS

Chapter One: The Good Book?	7
Chapter Two: End Time Origins	11
Chapter Three: Audience Relevance	17
Chapter Four: The Last Days	29
Chapter Five: Mark Of The Beast - 666	37
Chapter Six: Secret Rapture Of The Church	43
Chapter Seven: The Antichrist	49
Chapter Eight: End Of The World	55
Chapter Nine: The End Times	59
Chapter Ten: Elements Destroyed	65
Chapter Eleven: The Second Coming	67
Chapter Twelve: Destruction Of God's Temple	71
Chapter Thirteen: Signs Of The Times	77
Chapter Fourteen: Abomination Of Desolation	85
Chapter Fifteen: Book Of Revelation	87
Chapter Sixteen: The Great Tribulation	95

Chapter Seventeen: These Last And Evil Days	99
Chapter Eighteen: The Thief In The Night	109
Chapter Nineteen: Armageddon	111
Chapter Twenty: Final Thoughts	115
For Deeper Study, Check Out:	118

CHAPTER ONE
THE GOOD BOOK?

The Bible is called the "Good Book," and the message inside is "The Gospel" or "Good News," so why does it seem to be filled with so much death and destruction? Is it possible that we may have misunderstood or misinterpreted some things from the Scriptures? In this book, we will take another look at The Book of Revelation, The Last Days, The Great Tribulation, The End of the World, and the End Times referred to in the Bible. We will also look into the Mark of the Beast, 666, the Great Tribulation period, the AntiChrist, the Secret Rapture of the Church, Armageddon, and much more. Maybe because of the worldwide pandemic we have just gone through, I'm continually running into people with horrible fears of the world coming to an end and about these being the Last Days or the End Times. During the pandemic, people tied the vaccine to the AntiChrist, the Mark of the Beast, and the Great Tribulation period. It's causing a lot of fear and anxiety, so I'm going to attempt to try to clear some things up through scripture. In this book, I'm not trying to make up your mind for you; I just want to present you with some ideas, maybe some alternative ways of looking at things, as I use the Holy Scriptures to make my points.

I will allow you to use your common sense, your faith as a praying Christian, and the Holy Spirit to decide what's true or false. This book consists of about 23 videos I did a few years ago on my YouTube channel called "*Us Crazy Christians.*" End Times book is not an exhaustive gathering of information on these topics. I try to give enough insight and scriptural context to help you see another view, possibly a better view according to the scripture. I list books to read at the end of this book if you want more information. I suggest you start with "Raptureless" by Dr. Jonathan Welton and "Revelation of Jesus Christ" by Dr. Lynn Hiles. These two are easier to understand than the other books on my list[in my opinion], and they go a lot deeper into these subjects than I do.

While reading or listening to this book, please have an open mind. Temporarily forget what your Bishop taught, what your Pastor preached, and what your praying Grandmother told you about these Last and Evil Days. Be open to seeing scriptures without any filters or opinions for a while.

Is the Bible really the "Good Book"? Maybe the Bible is similar to a baseball bat. You can use a baseball bat to hit a home run and bring joy and excitement to millions, or you can use that bat to hit someone over the head and destroy them. The bat isn't bad; it depends on how you view or use it. Could how we view the Holy Scriptures be the same way? I think so. Let's get into it.

CHAPTER TWO
END TIME ORIGINS

To those of us who were raised in church to fear the End Times, some examples of how we think will seem completely normal, while others may view our mindsets as over the top. For those who weren't raised in this religious fear, please allow me to give a little more insight into some of our thought processes. I remember back in the day, some years ago, when I used to sell life insurance. Most of the time when I attempted to sell life insurance to my fellow Christians at church, they always seemed to have hesitancy about buying life insurance because they would say things like, "The Rapture could happen any minute, why waste my time and money," "These are the Last Days and the end of the world," "Look at the signs of the times, can't you tell that's a waste of time to buy life insurance." "William, you should get out of that business and do something else.." I would get that same kind of response at times when I would talk to some Christians about putting money aside for their kid's college. Honestly, I didn't personally believe in the need for it myself because I did have a strong belief in the Rapture happening any day. I wasn't even doing those things in my life, but as a salesman, I had to present that idea to others. When I explained it to Christians, most of the time, they were like, why worry about college? "Jesus is coming back any minute; I doubt my kids will make it to college." I was disheartened only because I wanted the sale, but I completely understood their thinking because I thought the same way.

I've heard stories about people refusing to get married or have children because of what Jesus talked about in the gospel written by Matthew, about having children in those last and evil days. Jesus says, "Woe to those who are married or have children in those days." Is it possible that they are taking that out of context and applying it to their lives, then they end up dying at an old age, never getting married, and never having kids? I wonder how many children were stunted from greatness, from making a positive effect or changing the world by their parents believing that they had no future, at least no future on Earth. When did this kind of thinking start? Throughout church history, most Bible scholars and theologians had a similar view of the End Times, but it wasn't how we view it today.

According to church history, from about 30 AD until the 1500s, most First-Century churches had an optimistic view of the future. They believed that the kingdom of God was growing on the earth and would continue to grow and make the world better. Still, during the reformation of the 1500s, there began teachings that became new beliefs in the Rapture, the AntiChrist, as well as a seven-year global great tribulation period. Still, before the 1500s, none of those topics were viewed that way or taught the way they are now in our churches in this Western civilization. In the 1500s, during the Reformation, Martin Luther strongly criticized the Roman Catholic Church, and he called them *"the Whore of Babylon"*. Most reformers then considered the Pope the AntiChrist, and they called the Roman Catholic Church the Beast of Revelation. To counter this and to clear the Catholic Church and Pope from these accusations; There was a Catholic Priest named Francisco Ribera, and in 1585, he wrote a thesis, or commentary, about 500 pages long on the Book of Revelation. And in this thesis, he strategically placed the Rapture in the future. He placed what Daniel said, all the prophecies of Jesus, Matthew, and so on as being something that would happen in the future, therefore excluding the Roman Catholic Church and the Pope from possibly being the AntiChrist or the Beast talked about in the book of Revelation, etc... But prior to that period, the church and the teachers of the Bible did not teach a future rapture, and they didn't believe in a coming apocalypse. Ribera's teaching didn't gain any steam until the 1800s. In the 1800s, as the bible was being translated and shared with everyone, it was reprinted and shared everywhere. Some Bible translators took hold of what Ribera said in his Thesis and implemented it in the scriptures, and it began to gain worldwide acceptance. Let me reiterate once again that before that period of time, nearly all the First-Century Christians, from those Christians who walked with Jesus until more than a millennium and a half, or over 15 Centuries after his Crucifixion on the cross, had totally different beliefs and views of the Last Days, of the end time prophecies that Jesus,

Daniel and so forth preached. They didn't view it the way the majority of the church views it today. If you want a more detailed explanation, read Dr. Jonathan Welton's book "Raptureless." He gives excellent and more detailed information in that book.

I have to admit that my belief in the Rapture happening at any moment hindered my life and plans for my future, as well as plans for my children's future. I have to admit that truth, sadly. I pray this book frees you and your mind from these scriptural misunderstandings. We're just getting started; hold on tight.

CHAPTER THREE
AUDIENCE RELEVANCE

It's important to deal with audience relevance before jumping into the Mark of the Beast, the Great Tribulation, the AntiChrist, etc. Audience relevance is something that theologians, Bible scholars, and historians understand and incorporate in interpreting the Bible or any other historical documents. Still, I've learned that many Church folk don't understand it. So, we're going to break that down in this chapter. Audience relevance is the consideration of who the writer was talking to and the possible understanding the audience may have of what the author or the speaker was saying. I remember as a child in the 70s growing up in Detroit, it seemed like everybody called each other "blood," "what's happening blood," "what's going on blood," etc. Blood had a meaning, and we understood blood back then to mean bro, buddy, friend, homie, etc. Fast forward another decade, the 80s and 90s, and all of a sudden, gang culture is really big, and then it starts to be mentioned in hip-hop lyrics. Then, blood has a different meaning and begins to refer to gang members. It had a different meaning than the decade before, so saying blood in the 70s to that audience meant something different than saying blood in the 80s and 90s to a different audience.

Most of the time, the word bad means something negative. It was almost self-explanatory, but there was a period during the 80s and 90s when LL Cool J and Michael Jackson reinterpreted the word and gave it a totally different meaning, and all of a sudden, bad was good. An example would be, "That girl is bad," confusing older generations at the time. I remember explaining to my mother that calling a woman bad was a compliment after she asked me what Janet Jackson did wrong cause I said, "Janet is bad!" I totally meant it as a compliment; again, audience relevance matters: who are the writers talking to, and what would have made sense to the audience that was listening at the time. Those are important things to consider.

My favorite Bible story as a child was Joseph and his coat of many colors. I think the reason I related to it so strongly was because Joseph had dreams and visions of his future, and his family didn't necessarily support him or believe in him so he had to kind of hold on to those dreams for himself and eventually, everything he said, everything he spoke, everything he dreamed, happened. I felt like I had dreams and goals and saw myself as more than my family and friends saw me to be or become. So I related to that story, but one thing that confused me, and I didn't understand the full depth of it at the time, being so young. When Joseph told his dream to his parents, his dream consisted of the Sun, the Stars, and the Moon bowing to him. Immediately after he woke up and explained that dream to his father, mother, and brothers, they were instantly offended. But Why? He didn't say they bowed to him; he said the stars, the moon, and the sun bowed and worshiped him. I wondered why they would be so upset at him. If you read the story, immediately after explaining the dream, his family says, "Who are you?" "Who do you think you are, that your parents would bow to you, that your siblings would bow to you?" They instantly understood his words as symbolism. It was audience relevance in action. The family members understood he was talking in symbolic or apocalyptic language. It was a language common to the Hebrews, not only in that one instance but all through the Old Testament, and in many of the New Testament scriptures, they used that same language. But because we choose to take things written in scripture so literally, some things tend to get lost in translation. If Joseph's parents had taken his dream or words literally as we do now, they never would have been upset at Joseph, but because they totally understood the meaning of what he was saying, because they knew he was using symbolic language, they clearly understood his words and were understandably offended. This way of speaking and writing is seen throughout all the cultures. You can call it prophetic language, apocalyptic language, or symbolic language. Regardless of what title you give it, it was clearly understood by the First-Century Christians who read the Old and New Testaments.

I have a friend of mine who said, "William, I've been over to the Middle East a few times recently, and right now, if you go over to the Middle East you will notice they talk to each other in such dynamic ways. He said even a simple communication between two friends and they're talking about destroying each other and killing each other and wiping each other off the face of the planet, and they're not even in a serious argument or debate." They just talk with such strong, over-the-top language even now." I can't personally verify if that is true because I haven't experienced that myself. If I'm wrong, forgive me, I got it from somebody else, secondhand knowledge. Regardless, that is something to think about. Could it be common to use words like the stars, the moon, the Heavens, and the Earth as symbols and not literal? You can see this kind of apocalyptic language throughout the Bible, not just in the New Testament prophecies, not just in the book of Revelation but all through the Old Testament books. Consider this fact: even in prophecies that according to scripture already came to pass, in the preceding prophecy they would mention the destruction of the world and the earth-shaking and other big supernatural things but when the actual prophecy came to pass, according to scripture, it was nothing at all like that. It was just symbolic of something that happened — research for yourself. I gave an example of an audience relevance issue in one of my first videos on my *"Us Crazy Christians"* YouTube channel. The video was called *"Why did God abandon Jesus on the cross."* I talk about how when Jesus was nailed to the cross he cried out, "Eli, Eli, lama sabachthani" which means, "My God, my God, why hast thou forsaken me?" We Christians in this modern generation, us Western civilized Christians, look at that and we think Jesus was complaining to God, we think he was distraught that God had turned his back on him, but further research shows using audience relevance and context, that Jesus was just repeating a quote from the Psalmist King David and it was a positive quote. It was a famous song in the First Century for the First Century Jews and Christians. Jesus quoted the lyric at the beginning of a song that most people who heard Jesus's voice would recognize. That song would likely cause the hearers to start singing, that powerful song of triumph and deliverance. Even if at that moment they were too distraught to sing it, they would remember his words just like we do now but because of Audience relevance, they would remember the Victorious

Psalm of David as opposed to the misinterpreted and assumed neglect Jesus felt. Scripture repeatedly says that God will NEVER leave us nor forsake us, so Jesus couldn't have been abandoned. God was with Jesus on the Cross. For example, if I simply say the words without singing them, "Amazing Grace, how sweet the sound." I would gamble that at least 95% of you reading or listening to this audiobook would know the next few words if not the entire song. Let that marinate.

If you're interested, you can read David's entire song here or just go to the next chapter.

The entire song is in scripture and ends in power and triumph.

Psalm 22 (Amplified Bible): A Cry of Anguish and a Song of Praise. To the Chief Musician; set to [the tune of] Aijeleth Hashshahar (The Doe of the Dawn). A Psalm of David

1. [a]My God, my God, why have You forsaken me?
   Why are You so far from helping me
   and from the words of my groaning?

2. O my God, I call out by day, but You do not answer;
   And by night, I find no rest *nor* quiet.

3. But You are holy,
   O You who are enthroned in [the holy place where] the praises of Israel [are offered].

4. In You, our fathers trusted [leaned on, relied on, and were confident];
   They trusted, and You rescued them.

5. They cried out to You and were delivered;
   They trusted in You and were not disappointed *or* ashamed.

6. But I am [treated as] a worm [insignificant and powerless] and not a man;
   I am the scorn of men and despised by the people.

7. All who see me laugh at me *and* mock me;
   They [insultingly] open their lips, they shake their head, *saying*,

8. "He trusted *and* committed himself to the LORD, let Him save him.
   Let Him rescue him because He delights in him."

9. Yet You are He who pulled me out of the womb;
   You made me trust when on my mother's breasts.

10. I was cast upon You from birth;
    From my mother's womb, You have been my God.

11. Do not be far from me, for trouble is near;
    And there is no one to help.

12. Many [enemies like] bulls have surrounded me;
    Strong *bulls* of Bashan have encircled me.

13. They open wide their mouths against me,
    Like a ravening and a roaring lion.

14. I am poured out like water,
    And all my bones are out of joint.

My heart is like wax;
It is melted [by anguish] within me.

15. My strength is dried up like a fragment of clay pottery;
And my [dry] tongue clings to my jaws;
And You have laid me in the dust of death.

16. For [a pack of] dogs have surrounded me;
A gang of evildoers has encircled me,
They pierced my hands and my feet.

17. I can count all my bones;
They look, they stare at me.

18. They divide my clothing among the.m
And cast lots for my [b]garment.

19. But You, O LORD, do not be far from me;
O You my help, come quickly to my assistance.

20. Rescue my life from the sword,
My only *life* from the paw of the dog (the executioner).

21. Save me from the lion's mouth;
    From the horns of the wild oxen, You answer me.

22. I will tell of Your name to my countrymen;
    In the midst of the congregation, I will praise You.

23. You who fear the LORD [with awe-inspired reverence], praise Him!
    All you descendants of Jacob, honor Him.
    Fear Him [with submissive wonder], all you descendants of Israel.

24. For He has not despised nor detested the suffering of the afflicted;
    Nor has He hidden His face from him;
    But when he cried to Him for help, He listened.

25. My praise will be of You in the great assembly.
    I will pay my vows [made in the time of trouble] before those who [reverently] fear Him.

26. The afflicted will eat and be satisfied;
    Those who [diligently] seek Him *and* require Him [as their greatest need] will praise the LORD.
    May your hearts live forever!

27. All the ends of the earth will remember and turn to the LORD,
    And all the families of the nations will bow down *and* worship before You,

28. For the kingship *and* the kingdom are the LORD'S
    And He rules over the nations.

29. All the prosperous of the earth will eat and worship;
    All those who go down to the dust (the dead) will bow before Him,
    Even he who cannot keep his soul alive.

30. Posterity will serve Him;
    They will tell of the Lord to the next generation.

31. They will come and declare His righteousness.
    To a people yet to be born — He has done it [and it is finished].

CHAPTER FOUR
THE LAST DAYS

All over the world, In some colleges and other places that revere and observe history, they consider Jesus to be a false prophet. The reason is that they understand that when Jesus was speaking to or prophesying to people, he was speaking directly to the people in front of him and prophesying about them for their lifetime. Many people who teach at these institutes of learning or places that value the lessons of history believe that Jesus did exist and said many of the things he is quoted as saying, but because those things Jesus spoke of never came to pass, they view Jesus as a false prophet, which confirms in their minds his illegitimacy as the Son of God. Those historians, college professors, and students are astutely aware that Jesus clearly states in scripture, "These things will happen before this generation standing before him would pass." Jesus even said, "Some of you standing here or sitting here listening to me will not die or taste death till all of these things happen." Could Jesus Christ be a false prophet?

Or is it possible that everything Jesus prophesied would happen, did happen in the time frame he said it would happen? Let's look into it. Hebrews chapter 1, verses 1 and 2 says, "In these Last Days," confirming that the Last Days Jesus talked about were then, not now, or any time in the future. Again, He said, "In these Last Days," and that was over 20 centuries ago. Think about that. Scripture says, "God in these Last Days has spoken to us by his son Jesus." I know a natural reflex might have just gone off inside of your mind when I quoted that scripture because a lot of "*Us Crazy Christians*" (Also the title of my YouTube Channel) have a tendency to view the scriptures like they are speaking directly to us, ignoring audience relevance.

When Jesus said, "In these Last Days," He was talking to a specific people, at a particular time, in a particular place. Also, keep in mind that it says, "God hath in these Last Days." Hath is past tense, meaning already done. As a matter of fact, it's very possible that the book of Hebrews, where this scripture is found, was written about four to six years before all the prophecies that Jesus spoke about came to pass. Proving Jesus to be an amazingly accurate prophet. Consider this: Is it possible that all of Jesus Christ's talks about the end times or the end of the age coming happened in 70 AD? Acts chapter 2 verses 16 through 18, says that the Apostle Peter on the day of Pentecost said, "That they were in the Last Days that were spoken of." Peter said that over 2000 years ago, on the day of Pentecost. First, John chapter 2 verse 18 says, "It is the last time," not it's coming soon, but it is the last time now, back then. He also says you have heard it said that AntiChrist will come in the Last Days, in the last time, but many AntiChrist have come. That is how we know it is the last time, the Last Days, the last hour. In Matthew chapter 23, Jesus mentions a bunch of end-time woes; after that, in chapter 24, he says to his audience, standing in front of him, that all of these things will come upon you, this generation. Remember, we talked about audience relevance, and Jesus was clearly speaking to the people sitting or standing before him—those who were hearing his voice at that moment, at that time. A biblical generation is 40 years according to scripture, like when the scripture says the children of Israel were wandering in the wilderness for a generation that was 40 years according to scripture. Now we're going to Matthew 24. But I want to mention that I realize many people don't know that when the Bible was written, there were no chapters and verses back then, so chapter 24, which we're about to talk about, is a continuation of chapter 23. Chapters and verses were added centuries later. So, please remember that chapter 24 is a continuation of chapter 23. Jesus talks about all the woes and horrible things that are going to happen before that generation dies. Jesus is asked when all of these things will be. When will everything you talked about, all the woes, the end of the world, the great tribulation, the destruction of the Heavens and the Earth, the burning of the elements, etc? When is that going to happen? The disciples asked him when will the end come, when is the end of the world, and a sign of your coming. Jesus replies in chapter 24, "That this generation shall not pass until <u>all of those things be fulfilled."</u> Luke chapter 21 talks about why Jesus says woe unto those who have children that day.

Woe unto them who are with child in that day because of the wrath that is to come upon Israel. Then a little further on, Jesus says that all of these things will happen before this generation passes. Matthew chapter 16, verses 27 through 29, says, "For the son of man shall come in the glory of his father, with his angels, and then he shall reward

every man according to his works." Jesus then said, "Verily I say unto you that there are some of you standing here right now that should not taste death until all these things be fulfilled, until you see the son of man coming in his Kingdom." That also sounds like it could be tied to the great throne judgment that people talk about. Jesus said he was coming back to give every man according to his deeds. That sounds like the great day of judgment that is spoken of but he said that this will happen in some of your lifetimes who were standing with him then, unless you think there are men and women who stood in front of Jesus over 19 centuries ago that are still standing here today! If you believe that, then I can't argue with you. If you believe that possibility, then okay, I have no argument, or maybe you just believe Jesus was a liar and false prophet. I'd like to offer the idea or question, is it possible that we just simply misunderstood and took out a context, what the scriptures say? Jesus gave his prophecies about the destruction of the temple, the end of the world, the Last Days, the tribulation period, the woes, all the wars, and rumors of wars were stated by Jesus all in or around 30 a.d and within a generation just like he said 70 AD which was 40 years later exactly everything he prophesied was fulfilled and it's historically documented and you can go check it out for yourself. It's a fascinating and eye-opening read.

Now the reason that most of the church is not so keen on Jewish history is because it's not in the canon of scripture. Anything written past the book of Revelation or the book of Hebrews and we tend to ignore it and invalidate it. We think the only thing that's valid for us is the scriptures but simple research, not even an exhaustive search into Jewish history will show you all about 70 AD and how all of Jesus's prophecies were fulfilled, all of them! Daniel's prophecy and the prophecies in the book of Revelation all fulfilled within a generation of the death, burial, and resurrection of Jesus, just as he said it would. In AD 70 according to historical documents the temple was destroyed with not one stone being left upon another just like Jesus said. The whole Jewish system was destroyed and eradicated. There were no more sacrifices for sins. You either accepted Jesus as the new sacrifice for sins, or your sins could not be forgiven because you had no temple to go to offer

your sacrifices. After all, it was burned to the ground and destroyed. Destroyed with the Temple was the old law system, the Ten Commandments, and the levitical record of who could become priests, and all of them that led the temple were killed.

Burnt offerings died in 70 AD. These are some facts, there were people who stood in front of Jesus and heard his words of the last days and end times who were still alive 40 years later and were there to see the destruction of the temple that Jesus had prophesied about. As a matter of fact, according to historical documents, the Jewish historian Josephus wrote that the followers of Jesus and the believers in Jesus fled the city and there's no documented record of any of them dying in a siege of 70 AD. That is because Jesus warned them and said when you see these things happening run for the heels and they obeyed and hid in the mountain. They were saved because they listened to Jesus talking directly to them about their lives, not our lives over 2000 years later. I just want to present some ideas to you, some things for you to pray about, meditate on, and research for yourself to make your own decisions.

CHAPTER FIVE
MARK OF THE BEAST - 666

We read about the a terrible ruler called the Beast and the Mark of the Beast represented by the number 666, in the book of Revelation. The Prophet Daniel also speaks about the Beast, but I wonder could the Beast terminology be referring to the Roman Empire that was lording over Israel at the time? Let's look into it. Scripture says, "The Beast shall ascend out of the pit," etc… It says, "The Beast has seven heads and sits on seven mountains." It's historically proven that the kingdom of Rome sat on seven mountains. Interesting. The book of Revelation mentions that the Beasts had seven heads and that they were seven kings. Now if you check Roman history or even biblical history, look into all the Julian Caesar's from 49BC till the destruction of the temple in 70 AD.

You will see that the timeline, as well as their length of reigns coincide with the scriptures' prophecy in the book of Revelation. While John was writing the book of Revelation on the Isle of Patmos, he wrote, "Five have fallen but one is." The one who is or was at the time, the current Julian Caesar who would have been ruling Rome at the time of the book of Revelation was Nero. Nero's name has a numerical value of six six six, 666. History of Nero records that he would dress up like a Beast and wear animal skin clothes on him. He was called the Beast at the time of that writing so again audience relevance makes sense meaning the readers of the book of Revelation at that time would have known precisely who John was talking about when he referenced the Beast unlike us 2000 years later. History says that Nero declared himself the Almighty God and demanded that everyone worship him. They were ordered to bow and worship him or suffer death. Nero persecuted Christians like crazy as he would have them lit on fire and watch them burn as he walked through his garden. Nero set up a statue of himself and ordered the people to worship it, burning incense on the statue. To his image, which the people called the image of the Beast. After the people finished burning incense at the image of the statue of the Beast, then the priests or the soldiers would use the ash from the burnt incense to place a Mark on their forehead or their right hand that allowed them to go and buy or sell in the Marketplace. But without that Mark, you could not buy or sell anything. Does that Sound familiar? It reminds me of every Rapture or End times movie I've ever seen. But this did happen already, yet we are still in fear of it happening to us now. I lived in fear and anxiety for decades from all of those end-time movies that churches have produced over the years? But I have to admit that those scary movies did frighten a bunch of people to say the sinners prayer over the years. With that said, I wonder if you are frightened into relationships is that a real genuine relationship? Can love come from fear? Possibly, but I wouldn't want to be in a relationship were someone is with me only out of fear for their life.

How about you?

As I was growing up, I remember hearing Preachers, Apostles, Prophets, and bible study teachers repeatedly talking about how one day they're going to try to give us a chip in our hand or a chip in our forehead and put the Mark of Beasts on us. If we don't deny Jesus Christ and Worship the Beast we can't eat and stuff like that. I taught that same belief myself for many years. I think I even taught that to my children, so I'm not poking fun or picking on anybody. I believed in this stuff myself; I've heard it myself for many years. But is it possible that again we've just overrun our imagination and made up things to be future tense when in all actuality they are past tense? Let's keep looking.

When the First Century Christians would say Jesus is Lord it wasn't on the same level of intensity as how we say Jesus is lord now because to say Jesus is lord back then was considered treasonous. Nero would have you tortured and then murdered for saying that Jesus was Lord. Nero the Beast was the Almighty God and you could not worship any other God but Nero. Nero eventually had his image placed on the money and the money with the image of the Beast or Nero was the only money you could use in the Marketplace. No other currency was accepted. So to buy, sell or to eat, you had to use the money with the Mark of the Beast. This all happened around about 64 AD through 68 AD. Again when talking about this Great Tribulation period, when the church would be persecuted it was said that these things must shortly come to pass. Not still waiting over 2000 years later. Why are we still waiting for these things to happen in the future? Let's consider the possibility that the Beast of the book of Revelation represented Rome, the head of the Beast was represented at that moment in history by the Julian Caesar Emperor Nero, and the seven heads were the seven Julian Caesars who surrounded Nero. Five before Nero and one after Nero. Jesus mentioned the significant period of great tribulation for believers. If you search history, you will learn that Nero was one of the greatest enemies to the body of Christ. History documents in fact that Nero set Rome on fire himself and blamed the Christians in order to have Christians all over the world martyred and killed. This is the historical fact of exactly what happened. Research this for yourself.

CHAPTER SIX
SECRET RAPTURE OF THE CHURCH

The secret pre-tribulation Rapture of the church has always been one of my favorite things to learn about for decades but I did not know that there is absolutely not even one verse of scripture in the Bible that mentions the Rapture. Wow! If you study the history of our common view of the Rapture and the End Times you will discover that the way that we view it today wasn't taught by anyone in church history up until the 1500s and that was widely ignored until the 1800s. In the 1800s, they began to print out Bibles on a mass scale to try to have everyone have their own Bible and those translators and bible printers took the idea of one man in the 1500s and put that in their printed literature of the Bible. Those interjections into New Testament scriptures are what led to the widespread belief in the current Rapture and end-time beliefs most of the church holds today. But again before that, the early church fathers and the early First Century Christians had an opposite view of the End Times and the Rapture. There are four passages in scripture that people use to teach this Rapture idea. Let's get into it.

First Thessalonians chapter 4 verses 13 through 18, says, "We will be caught up together with them in the clouds to meet the lord in the air." In recorded history and even in the context of this scripture, you can see that Paul was talking to the Thessalonian church about the great suffering and persecution they were currently experiencing. Paul even says as much in that same letter. Members of the Thessalonian church had been murdered because of their faith, which is what Paul was referring to as being resurrected as Jesus was resurrected. This was not about a secret Rapture seven years before the final judgment but It does seem possible that Paul is talking about the final judgment, when the books are opened and people are judged for their works, etc.. Let me make an additional point about this scripture. A lot of us currently view the word air as a reference to the sky but the literal Greek word refers to our atmosphere or the air we breathe that surrounds us, on the Earth. Also, consider the fact that the higher we go in the sky the less air there is. It is a fact that If you go high enough you will suffocate and die. The term, where it says in scripture, "caught up to meet the lord." In Greek, it refers to greeting someone, like Hello nice to meet you. Think about that. We tend to view the term, "caught up" as being lifted up in the sky, but in the Greek, it means "to catch up." For example, if you're walking down the street with your child and your child runs ahead of you and you say hey stop and you catch up to your child, that is what it means. Not caught up in the air. Scripture says that Christ will be equally yoked with his bride, the church. Meaning he will be equally yoked with *"Us Crazy Christians"*. So could this scripture be referring to us catching up to Christ, his likeness, his image in the earth, his glory, and his holiness? Is this what scripture is referring to about us being, "transformed in a moment, in a twinkling of an eye?" I think so. We are to be equally yoked as the bride of Christ then we will meet or greet Jesus on earth, in this atmosphere. Think about it. Matthew chapter 24 verses 40 through 42 mentions. "Two men in the field, one will be taken another left." "Two women grinding at the mill, one will be taken, another left." History shows on record, that there were random killings by the Romans in the siege on Jerusalem in 70 AD. The entire End Time prophecy that Jesus is talking about in Matthew 24 is about the destruction in 70 AD. On top of all of that, Jesus said that all of these things mentioned, "two men in the field one taken, two women at the meal, one taken." That all of that and all the other stuff he mentioned would happen before the generation of individuals who standing before him would pass. Another verse of scripture used to promote the idea of a Secret End Time Rapture of the Church is in the book of Revelation chapter 4 verse 1. It says, "A door opened in Heaven with a voice saying, come up here." People equate that and use that in reference to the Rapture but in the context of scripture it's clear to see that John was talking about something that had happened to himself. Although John's body was still imprisoned on the Isle of Patmos, his spirit and mind were caught up in the upper Heavens to be shown things by Jesus. Which he then wrote about. He was talking about himself and his spiritual situation, not the Rapture of the church. In Revelation chapter

12 verse 5, it talks about "the Child being caught up to God and his throne." But that is referring to the ascension of Christ, not the church. Which explains why Child is capitalized. It is talking about Jesus and that's even more clear if you read it in context. To scripturally believe in the Rapture Theory, we have to use our imagination, we have to flex our minds to the truth of scripture and use verses out of context to arive at any type of clear understanding of the Rapture idea. To make these scriptures fit into that paradigm or theory requires a lot of assumptions and make-believe. I'm honestly a little embarrassed by my strong belief and years of teaching something so loosely imagined from scripture. That is a testament to how opinions shared from the pulpit or the local church can blur our reading of the Bible and its scriptures. If we just simply read scripture in context as the writer meant, we would see they are not talking about any kind of Rapture of the church. No wonder most of the church is still waiting over 2000 years later for the words of Jesus to manifest. Let it marinate. I encourage you to read these verses again, research them for yourself in

context without any preconceived notions, theories, or ideas, and let the truth speak for itself. Allow the Holy Spirit to bring the truth alive and you use your common sense Christianity to decide the truth. If you would like a more detailed and in-depth study about the Rapture, I encourage you to read Dr. Jonathan Welton's book "Raptureless". It will bless you. It's a great read and much more detailed than I am in this chapter. I hope this blessed you and I hope it freed you. Stick with me, we have more to uncover.

CHAPTER SEVEN
THE ANTICHRIST

The current idea of a one world leader or AntiChrist, possessed by Satan himself, that is commonly taught today comes from a compilation of only four scriptures in the Bible. Allow me to interject that because it seems that when people refer to the AntiChrist they're always talking about the book of Revelation in connection with the AntiChrist but the word AntiChrist is not used at all, not even one time in the entire book of Revelation. Research it for yourself. But it is found three times in First John and one time in Second John. I want to hit a few different points but first, let's deal with context. In the context of John's letter, he is talking to or about believers who have denied that Jesus had come in the flesh. There was a religious sect of people who were at that time claiming that Jesus was not a man but only a spirit. This is why John seems to go out of his way to mention how Jesus was the word that became flesh and dwelt among us. John went on in his epistle to say that those who claim that

Jesus did not have a physical body were AntiChrist or against Christ Jesus. He said, "Many false prophets have come, and everyone that acknowledges that Jesus has come in the flesh is from God, but every spirit that denies that Jesus came in the flesh is not from God, and this is the spirit of AntiChrist." You can read that in First John chapter four, verses one through three. Second John chapter one verse seven says, "many deceivers who do not acknowledge Jesus as coming in the flesh have gone out into the world and any such person is a deceiver and the AntiChrist." The second point I'd like to mention is that the term, "the AntiChrist" is not found in the original greek. AntiChrist is only capitalized because "the" was falsely inserted causing AntiChrist to be considered a proper noun but that was not so in the original greek. The "the" wasn't added until the 1500s during the reformation period when the protestants were at odds with the catholic church. In the original translation, it is simply AntiChrist which refers to a belief or a way of thinking. It was never referring to an actual person or one world leader. Martin Luther and the Protestant movement were attacking the catholic church and the pope. They were publicly labeling them the Beast of Revelation and the AntiChrist. So they added the "the" to make their complaints or charges more legitimate against the catholic church. In 1st John chapter 2 verses 20 through 23, John says, "Who is the liar? It is whoever denies that Jesus is the Christ. Such a person is the AntiChrist." According to scripture, the Children of Israel had known the spirit of AntiChrist was coming; they were expecting there to be teachings or beliefs that came against the messiah, the Christ but they were never expecting the coming of one world leader, possessed by Satan to take over the world. They knew the AntiChrist as a false teaching or a religious movement but not as a specific person. Many of Us Crazy Christians use Daniel chapter 9 verses 24 through 27 to get much of our information on the AntiChrist but there's no mention of an AntiChrist figure in Daniel chapter 9. Most Bible commentaries before the 1500s believe that Daniel chapter 9 was then referring to the future coming messiah Jesus Christ. This is not 2nd William chapter two [*I didn't make this up, it's in the Bible*], you can go research this for yourself.

Second Thessalonians chapter two, mentions the "man of lawlessness who exalts himself over everything that is called God. Who sets himself up as God to be worshiped." He sets himself up in God's temple proclaiming to be God, the scripture says. That is impossible to happen in our future the temple was destroyed in 70 AD. From that day to now, centuries later, no other temple has even been built and there are no plans for any future temples as a matter of fact there are no scriptures, not even one that speaks of a future temple being built on earth. So if this AntiChrist is coming in the future, where is this man of sin the scripture talks about going to stand and proclaim himself God? In what temple? If you read the Jewish historian Josephus's account of the siege of Jerusalem in 70 AD. He writes that in the destruction of the temple, a man by the name of John Levy seems to fit the description of the man of lawlessness. In 70 AD John Levy took over the temple and proclaimed himself as God and as Savior and he did many other things that fit the man of lawlessness predictions or prophecies perfectly. Now that I'm more mature in my knowledge and simple common sense, it doesn't make sense to me logically that Paul would have written a letter that would have absolutely no value or purpose for the readers who were in imminent danger. Think about that. On the other hand, if these things were to happen within a generation like Jesus said. That would mean possibly within 10 years or less from when Paul wrote that letter, all those atrocities warned about would happen. That would make more sense. But to imagine that he was writing that letter to them and sending it to them and it still hasn't happened. It never happened to them and their generation, it didn't happen to their kids, and still hasn't happened to us! That makes absolutely no sense at all. Why write and warn those people about an occurrence that won't have any effect on their lives or the lives of their children but ignore entirely the life-altering destruction that would happen in about ten years from his letters? Let it marinate, think about it, pray about it. Maybe there will never be a demon-possessed, one world leader in our future. Perhaps the gospel is spreading and changing the world for the better just as prophesied. Maybe Jesus, John, Daniel, and Paul were very accurate and timely Prophets. I think so. What do you think?

CHAPTER EIGHT
END OF THE WORLD

Continuing with our End Times Book on the Last Days. In the chapter titled End Time Origins, we talked about how we came to this point of belief through scripture. Then we dealt with a very important chapter called Audience Relevance and how it matters in what was said and who it was said to and how they interpreted what was said. In the next chapter, we're going to jump into the End Times but in this chapter, I want to deal with the few scriptures that talk about The End Of The World. Nearly every Biblical Theologian, Bible scholar or Historian understands and agrees that The King James Version, misinterpreted the word "world" when it was translated from the Greek to the King James Version. Instead of saying "end of the world," it should correctly say "end of the age" or the "end of an era". That would be the literal Greek definition in translation of the original Greek word. This is even more proven by the fact that almost every other biblical translation besides the King James Versions uses "end of the age" as opposed to "end of the world". Don't take my word for it, research it for yourself. In First Corinthians chapter 10, verse 11. Paul was speaking to the Corinthian church and he said to them that they are the people to whom the end of the world has come. Hebrews chapter 9, verses 25 through 28 talks about how "Jesus hath at the end of the world put away sin." "Hath," is past tense, meaning he already did it, and it says he did it at the end of the world. That could be confusing, but when you come to realize that the literal translation of the word "world" in the Greek means age or era the confusion dissipates. There are several scriptures throughout the Bible that explain that the earth will last forever. Deuteronomy chapter 4 and verse 40 says, "The earth which the lord thy God giveth thee is forever." Psalms chapter 37 and verse 29 says, "The righteous shall inherit the land and dwell there forever." Psalms chapter 78 and verse 69 says, "the earth he has established forever." The last one I'll give is Psalms chapter 104 verse 5, "Who laid the foundations of the earth, that it should not be removed forever." That doesn't sound like the world is going to end to me. So I hope that clears up the end of the world scriptures for you and trust me we'll get into the verses mentioning the destruction of the Heavens and the earth and the elements but in the next chapter, we're going to deal with those scary end-time scriptures stick around.

CHAPTER NINE
THE END TIMES

Is it possible that the End Times was talking about an event that was approaching the First Century church or the First Century Christians and is currently in our past? Let's examine it. In the book of Daniel, Daniel's end-time prophecy, talks about a lot of the same things that Jesus prophesied about but God tells Daniel to seal up the prophecies he received because they are "not near", they are "far off". Think about that. But in contrast, in the New Testament, concerning Jesus's prophecies, John's prophecies in the book of Revelation, and Paul and Peter's prophecies, they all say the "end is near," "It's coming soon" or "shortly," et cetera. As a matter of fact in the book of Revelation, John is told to "not seal up the book because the time is near, the time is at hand." Completely different command than Daniel received for his similar prophecies being that they were far off. Seems that even God follows audience relevance.

Habakkuk 2 says, "that the vision of the End Times is for an appointed time, and though it will take a while wait for It." Again Habakkuk is an Old Testament prophet, many years before Jesus was ever born, and when he's given his end-time prophecy, he is told to wait for it although it may take awhile. Juxtapose that to the New Testament prophecies, all of which say, "coming soon," "this generation," "shortly," "at hand," "at the door," or "near." In Hebrews chapter 10, verse 37 it quotes the same verse in Habakkuk. But changes it up a little bit by saying in the New Testament, "in a little while" as opposed to in Habakkuk, "wait for it, although it may tarry and take a while." Revelation chapter 22 verses 6 through 7 says, "All these things will shortly be done." If you move on to verse 12 it says, "Behold I come quickly." James chapter 5 verses 8 and 9 says, "The coming of the lord draws nigh, the judge standeth before the door." Being at the door is an example of just how close he really was. He was at the door. First Peter chapter 4 and verse 7 says that "the end of things are at hand."

Revelation Chapter 1 verse 1 says, "to show those things which must shortly or soon come to pass." Verse 3 says, "The time is near or at hand." All of these New Testament verses mentioning soon, quickly, shortly, at hand, or near were all written over 19 centuries ago. Think about that. Many of Us Crazy Christians still believe they haven't happened yet. If that's true then Jesus, John, Peter and a lot of the Bible writers are absolute liars and false prophets or maybe they've simply been misunderstood or misinterpreted and taken out of context.

Another nail in the coffin, that really woke me up during my studies. This was how the literal Greek words for soon, shortly, quickly, and at hand are used all over the Bible in different instances, outside of end-time prophecies. And in every case they happened quickly, fast, in a hurry, momentarily, etc… but because we have a different view of the end-times, something that was preached to us or taught to us or misunderstood by us we ignore those obvious and timely uses throughout scripture. We ignore logic and common sense by interpreting "soon or quickly" as meaning that it could be a lot longer even many centuries longer than what soon or quickly means. The best argument I ever heard to explain why soon, quickly, at hand, shortly, etc.. didn't mean what we thought it meant and I've used this same argument as well for decades myself. That argument is in Second Peter chapter three, verse eight, where it says, "that a thousand years are as one day with the lord." I leaned heavily on that scripture to overcome the overwhelming use of soon in scripture. The problem with that belief or theory is that, you have to use your imagination and use scripture out of context to make that fit.

Maybe this particular verse of scripture is simply explaining that God is not limited by natural processes of time. God is outside of time. He Created time. But He knows that us humans, His creation or His children don't view time that way. Maybe God is wise enough to communicate important information to creation in a way that they can understand it. Maybe God knows how we view the difference between soon and a long time or the difference between quickly and slowly. Maybe? Please forgive my sarcasm and please believe me when I say I was thinking of myself as I was writing that. I'm kinda embarrassed at myself.

Remember as stated before, almost every Biblical Theologian, Bible Scholar, and Biblical Historian clearly understands that the end of the world was mistranslated in the King James Version and it literally means the end of the age or an end of an era. Although many of the Bible Theologians, Scholars, etc.. may disagree on exactly when that era or that age began. To cancel all argument, we can simply take the furthest distance of time that anybody can agree on which begins at Adam and ends at Jesus, that is the longest era that anybody can agree on, there's no longer era really than that. If we use that era of time as the Old Covenant or the Old Testament. The old era began with Adam but a lot of people believe it started actually with Moses regardless let's go further back, let's start with Adam through the timeline up until Jesus. Once Jesus is on the scene, He then, and so does every Apostle, Prophet, and Bible writer after him say that "the end is near," "the end is now," "it is at hand," or "it is coming quickly". Are we to believe that the end they were referring to, we are still waiting on it almost 20 centuries later and still the clock is ticking? Where in the history of the world in any circumstance or situation is the end of something, many, many times longer than the thing itself? Think about it. So the era that scripture says is ending at its longest period of existence is not even half that amount of time as its ending? And keep in mind many of us Church folk are still waiting for it to happen. To make sure to clarify so we are on the same page. Is it wise to believe that the ending of a book is many times longer than the book itself? Or that the ending of a movie is much longer than the entirety of the movie? Absolutely not. That doesn't even make logical sense. Let's use our common sense Christians, pray about it, meditate on it, research it for yourself, and decide for yourself. Again I'm not trying to make up your mind for you, I just want to present some ideas, some new thoughts, plant some seeds and if there is fertile ground, if it makes sense to you, it will grow. If not, throw it aside. No big deal. I don't have any problem being wrong. I've been wrong before. Like I said I preached and taught the popular view of the End Times to many people, even to my own children without knowing I was wrong.

CHAPTER TEN
ELEMENTS DESTROYED

The Bible talks about the very elements around us being destroyed. In 2nd Peter chapter 3 verses 10 and 12. It says twice that the elements will melt with fervent heat. Was Peter referring to the elements of earth wind and fire or the elements of the Periodic Table that were created about 1800 years after he died? Probably not. Was he instead talking about the destruction of the elements that contain the laws of Judaism like the stone tablets that were housed in the temple that was destroyed in the fire of 70 AD? The Greek word Peter uses for elements is "stoicheia" which means the rules or laws. That word only appears a few times in the New Testament. Galatians chapter 4 mentions it twice. Colossians chapter 2 mentions it twice and Hebrews chapter 5 mentions it once. If you read those verses you will see that each one is referring to the law, the rules, the principles of Judaism, or the Ten Commandments. Think about that for a minute and also consider that some of those verses mention being in bondage under those elements and there are scriptures elsewhere that mention being in bondage under the law. Notice the similarities? Quick side note. Peter also mentions in the same passage that the earth and the things built on it will be burned up and destroyed. The first thing I want to mention about that is how the Greek word for Earth in that verse means "land" and not the planet earth so in context it is saying that the land in Jerusalem that the temple is built upon will be burned and destroyed. Which according to historical accounts is exactly what happened in 70 AD. Hope this brings you, Peace.

CHAPTER ELEVEN
THE SECOND COMING

There is only one verse of scripture that alludes to the second coming of Jesus Christ. It is in Hebrews chapter 9 verse 28 and it says, "so Christ was once offered to bear the sins of many and unto them that look for him he shall appear a second time without sin unto salvation." Again this is the only verse to even hint at a second coming and it doesn't even say "the second coming". It seems like we have reworded it to say what we had already previously believed or had been taught to believe but it is obvious through both Old and New Testament scriptures that Jesus came and went many times throughout scripture. The second coming of Jesus Christ in the way that we view it or most of the church views it, is likely misinterpreted or out of context. Let's look into it. The very next verse in chapter 10, where the scripture calls the temple, the priest, and the burnt offerings a shadow of the things to come.

All the verses before Hebrews Chapter 9 and verse 28, and all the verses of the next chapter immediately after all are talking about the high priest of the temple and the temple sacrifices. You have your Bible, go on and Read it yourself. It mentions how they were types and shadows of what Jesus came to do and did do. It mentions that after the burnt offerings and the sacrifices were made by the priest, those same sacrifices never removed the Children of Israel's sins for good but only for a moment. It says that when they took a second look they would notice and see that their sins still existed. It says they would see their sins again. But because of Jesus's sacrifice for sin being eternal, when they look again at Jesus a second time they will see that no more sacrifice for sins is needed because they are forgiven eternally and they will see their sins no more. Jesus covered all of their sins and all of our sins, once and for all with his blood. Unlike the temple sacrifices that only lasted for a moment. They were temporary sacrifices but Christ's sacrifice was eternal. That is the Good News!! Again this is not 2nd William chapter two [I am not cooking up stories]. You have your Bible, you can research it for yourself.

The Second Coming was not talking about the Second Coming of Jesus Christ to the earth. Jesus had come and gone many times according to scripture, also according to the scripture he currently resides on the inside of us. Why would he need to come back anywhere? He never left, so how could he come back? Is scripture lying or mistaken by saying Christ is inside of us? Is it possible that we've taken that scripture out of context or simply misunderstood it? Allow me to bring your attention to one more issue, historically, with the temple sacrifices. The sacrifices were not always guaranteed to work. Temple servants or other Priests would normally have to tie a rope with a bell and attach it to the High Priest as he entered into the Holy of Holies to see if the sacrifices would be accepted by God or not. If God did not accept them the Priest would be killed and because no one could just enter into the Holy of Holies they would have to pull his dead body out by the rope that they had tied to him if they no longer heard the bell ringing. So the crowd or the audience [*the children of Israel*] sat in bated breath, anxious and nervous, hoping with their fingers crossed that God would accept their sacrifice, so their sins would be forgiven but only temporarily. They had to do it all again every year. But Jesus Christ died once, and he died for all sins.

The old age or the Old Covenant and the old way of doing things by blood sacrifice, the temple, and the law according to scripture have been made obsolete. Thank you, Jesus! I Hope this chapter blesses you and added some clarity or confirmation.

CHAPTER TWELVE
DESTRUCTION OF GOD'S TEMPLE

I on purpose repeat myself in these chapters for two reasons. First, because all of these chapters are tied together by one central idea that needs to be reiterated. Secondly, I know many people will likely not read this book in the order it is presented but instead will go to the topic they are most intrigued about. So I have to repeat some things for that chapter to make sense. So please bear with me. I appreciate you!

Scripture mentions that Jesus said, "When you see Jerusalem surrounded by enemies, flee to the mountains." In the siege of 70 AD according to historical records, there was a period when the Roman armies halted their attack and pulled back for a certain period of time and the Christians, the believers remembered the signs of the End Times that Jesus prophesied and his instruction to flee to the mountains and they did exactly that. Josephus the Jewish/Roman Historian stated in his writings that not one believer of Jesus Christ is recorded as dying in the siege of 70 AD because they fled just as Jesus had warned them to. Honestly, I could go on and on with so much information about 70 AD but I didn't want this to be a large book, filled with many quotes and scriptures. I want to do more idea planting and encourage you to study for yourself. If you study 70 AD you will see that every prophecy that Jesus gave about the end of the world, the end of the age was fulfilled in 70 AD. Peter prophesied that the elements

melted with a fervent heat and in our current language we think the elements are like earth wind and fire or mercury, copper, etc.. but context is key and that's why audience relevance is so important because back then elements meant the law of Moses, the law that was written on the tablets, the ten commandments, the tablets of the law of Moses were in the temple which was destroyed and burned down with one stone not left upon the other, in the siege and attack of 70 AD. That is a historical fact you can verify. In second Peter chapter 3, verse 10, he says, "The Heavens will pass away." And in truth, the Heavens and Earth did pass away. They were burned to the ground, they still don't exist to this day! How is that possible William? It's just more symbolic language. The Jewish Historian Josephus explains that the

Heavens and the Earth were representative of the temple. The Israelites, the Hebrews, the Jewish people of that time considered the Outer Court the Earth, and the Inner Court, or the Holy of Holies was representative of the Heavens. So when Jesus said tear this temple down and I'll rebuild i've heard some brilliant Preachers explain that Jesus was talking about His body being crucified and I'll conceed that its highly possible Jesus had a double meaning but if we look in context coupled with audience relevance, it was clear that the scribes and pharasies understood his meaning and were furious at his word. Regardless of that, when Jesus said the Heavens and Earth shall pass away. He was still talking about the temple, which passed away in 70 AD. The Jewish people, the Israelites, hearing and reading these things, would have known what Jesus was talking about without confusion. Why do you think they were so offended and mad at Jesus? How dare you threaten their temple with its representation of heaven and earth. Hebrews chapter 9 calls the Inner Court or the Holy of Holies, inside the temple, "the Heavens," but it calls it a fake Heaven or a symbolic Heaven representing the true Heaven or Holy of Holies that Jesus would enter for us, to save us from our sins. The temple was simply a type and a shadow of what was to come in Jesus. This is not an exhaustive study of the siege of 70 AD; this is just an attempt to give you some things to think about that may pique your interest and cause you to want to study and research more if you're interested. Please allow me to throw some common-sense Christianity in front of you before I'm done. Jesus's end-time prophecy spoke of the destruction of the temple of God and the creation and rebuilding of a new and better temple. Several verses mention how we are the temple of God. How God, Jesus, and the Holy Spirit now live on the inside of us in the new Temple. So with that in mind why are we still waiting for a new temple to be built? Think about it, also consider the scriptural fact that God never wanted a temple built in the first place. It was a man-made decision, a human decision, that God finally said okay to. The major purpose of the temple built back then was to have a place where the Children of Israel's sins could be forgiven by offering burnt offerings and sacrifices up to God in that temple for the forgiveness of their sins. So should we honestly believe that Jesus is coming back to build another temple, so we can offer up more blood sacrifices and offerings for our sins? Jesus already forgave us for all of our sins and our slate is wiped clean, by His sacrifice on the Cross! Just imagine even if it's true that Jesus Christ was coming back to create a new temple on earth, a place where He will reside as opposed to residing in us. Why should we be excited about that? Would that be good news or the gospel, to think that God is going to vacate us and go be in a place or location maybe in Jerusalem where we gotta go fly to him, to go wait in line to see him, to visit him, to have a word with him, to talk with him, to wait the long period to get past all the other billions of people who want to see God sitting in the temple? Can you imagine us being happy about that? Can you imagine that being exciting in reality? Can you imagine that, being a great future for us? To believe all of a sudden that we are no longer good enough for God to reside in and with and He has to go build him a temple and we can no longer have an intimate relationship with God on the inside of us wherever we are, wherever we go. But instead, we have to go find him in a temple in Jerusalem somewhere. Think about it. I hope this gives you some things to think about. I hope it brings you some joy, some peace, and some understanding.

CHAPTER THIRTEEN
SIGNS OF THE TIMES

"In France, a skinny man died of a big disease with a little name, by chance his sister came across a needle and soon she did the same, at home, there are 17-year-old boys and their idea of fun, is being in a gang called the disciples

high on crack toting a machine gun." "Sign of the Times," a great song by Prince. As entertaining as that song is, it is the actual signs of the times that bring much fear, dread, and anxiety to religious people all over the globe. Matthew Chapter 24 talks about the destruction of the temple and the signs of the End Times. It says, "There will be wars and rumors of wars," a great tribulation, the sun darkened, stars fall from Heaven, and Heaven and Earth will pass away. All of those seem like terrifying and horrible signs of the End of the World. But then Jesus says, "All of these things will happen before this generation passes." In another chapter, we talked about how long a generation is. According to scripture, a generation is 40 years and true to form in 70 AD which was 40 years after Jesus's prophecy. All of these things happened with the destruction of the temple, in the siege of Israel in 70 AD. We won't go through that again in this chapter because we've done it in other chapters. Is it possible that all of the signs of the times were fulfilled? The wars and rumors of wars can be proven historically that they happened. Jesus said you will be persecuted for my name's sake. There's so much historical documentation of Christians being murdered, martyred, and tortured for not denying or not turning away from Christianity, it's overwhelming. What about the earthquakes mentioned in the scriptures? Historical documents can verify that happened to Israel around that same time. Scripture talks about the elements being burned, again audience relevance matters. We look at elements right now and we're thinking of mercury, sulfide, etc, you know all the different elements but the literal definition of elements back then were considered the Law, the Ten

Commandments, and the tablets that the law was written on. They were stored inside of the Temple and when the temple was burned to the ground and not one stone was left upon another, those elements that were in the temple were destroyed as well, just as Jesus prophesied that the elements would be destroyed. He said that Heaven and Earth would be destroyed. Heaven and earth were symbolized in the temple. There are historical facts about that. There's even a scripture that alludes to that. Heaven and Earth were also destroyed when the temple was sacked and burned to the ground in 70 AD. Scripture says many false prophets will come, check history, that happened. One sign of the End Times or sign of the end of the age mentions fathers against sons and mothers against daughters. It is another historical fact that many believers or Christians were turned in to be murdered and killed by their children, their parents, their relatives, their neighbors, by their friends. They were considered to be treasonous lawbreakers and you could be rewarded for turning them in to the Roman government. Those turned in were murdered and tortured all over the Roman Empire. Which was pretty much the world at that time in history. Again you can research this stuff for yourself. I'm not trying to convince you of anything. I'm not trying to argue or debate with you. I just want to give you an alternative view that represents Joy, Peace, Freedom, Redemption and Salvation and Good News like Jesus talked about. These End Times prophecies were supposed to bring the hearer Joy, Peace, and Freedom from Bondage. So the dread of it happening in our future doesn't even coincide with the message of the good news of Jesus Christ. Maybe I'm wrong. Search for yourself. One of the best arguments I've heard to rebut what I've said is, that Scripture says, "the gospel or the good news has to be preached in all the world before the end comes." So that is supposed to be evidence that the end hasn't come yet because we believe the Gospel of Jesus isn't everywhere on the planet yet. But several scriptures say that the gospel has been preached all over the world and this was done at the time of the Bible writers. I'm gonna give you two scriptures right now Colossians chapter 1 verses 5 and 6 says, "The gospel has come to you as it is in all the world." That was written to the Colossian church. Colossians chapter 1 verse 23 says, "that the gospel was preached unto every creature under Heaven."

Jewish historians Josephus and Eusebius both record that during the period of around 70 AD, there were many miraculous signs in the Heavens all around the world, especially in Jerusalem. I encourage you to go take some time and read some of the stuff they recorded, the signs and wonders, it's miraculous. One of the Historians, I think it was Josephus said, "These things will be considered fables and fiction if there were not so many overwhelming witnesses to these miraculous occurrences." They record stuff like chariots in the sky, running around in the clouds, and all kinds of crazy stuff that I can't even remember now. But when you read it they will give you goosebumps. I remember thinking to myself that these were not even Christians who might be swayed to lie to confirm Christ's prophecies. They were non-believers recording this history. These writers are people talking about natural phenomena that they witnessed. Simple Jewish historians. If you take the time to read their accounts of Jewish history around that period of 70 AD you will be amazed at how much of Jesus' prophecy they mentioned and say is fulfilled not even knowing that they're fulfilling Jesus's prophecy or mentioning the fulfillment of Jesus prophecy. They confirm almost everything Jesus said, word for word, with more details than Jesus gave because they're talking about seeing it happen. Where Jesus talked about great signs he didn't say exactly what those signs would be. Check it out for yourself. I want to reiterate that it is believed that neither Josephus nor Eusebius were believers; it seemed like they had kind of derogatory comments on Jesus. I did not read everything they wrote, so I may miss some things but you can research for yourself. I think Josephus mentioned Jesus as being a false prophet that many people followed or something like that. One of the historians did call him a man who caused a stir in Jerusalem and stuff like that. It seems as you read their writings that they are confirming the end-time prophecies of Jesus Christ and have no idea they're even doing it. Lastly, I believe it was Eusebius and Josephus who said in their writings that not one of the followers of Jesus Christ, not one of the believers died in the siege of 70 AD because they all fled to Mount Pella. The historians seemed surprised but isn't that exactly what Jesus told them to do when they see armies surrounding Jerusalem? Jesus told the audience who was standing and sitting in front of him, "When you see these things happen, run for the mountains." "Don't go back in your house, don't do it, go run, getaway, and you will be saved." History says they were saved. Is it possible that the signs of the times passed along with the end of the age of the Old Covenant law? Study, pray about it, and decide for yourself. I pray this blessed you just as it blesses me.

CHAPTER FOURTEEN
ABOMINATION OF DESOLATION

The abomination that brings desolation is mentioned in both the Old and the New Testaments. In Matthew chapter 24, verse 15, Jesus says, "When you see the abomination of desolation as spoken of by the prophet Daniel,

run to the mountains, don't go home and get clothes, don't go to your house, woe to those who are with child in that day, pray that it's not winter when this happens

but run to the heels." Daniel speaks of the abomination of desolation as a man who stands in the temple, he destroys Jerusalem, the temple, and its sacrifices. All of this is a documented historical fact that all happened in 70 AD. In Matthew only a few verses later Jesus said that this generation standing before him would not pass before all these things are fulfilled. The abomination that brings desolation sounds menacing but we have absolutely nothing to fear. It was completed and passed away many centuries ago. I pray this information brings you both peace, understanding, and joy.

CHAPTER FIFTEEN
BOOK OF REVELATION

As a child growing up in church, the book of Revelation used to give me nightmares.

After I became an Adult, one of my goals in life was to do a special effects movie of the book of Revelation and I still might do that one day. As I write this I am continually having to erase the s from the end of Revelations. I've got to remember, it's the book of Revelation, not Revelations. There is just one Revelation and that is the Revelation of Jesus Christ and we're going to talk about that. To read the book of Revelation was terrifying as a matter of fact as a young Christian I avoided it most of the time. I didn't start trying to read until I was much older, in my late 20s. It reads like something straight out of a science fiction horror movie. But is it possible that the book of Revelation is a book not to be feared, anxious, or worried about in the slightest? Maybe it's not talking about something that's coming to haunt us in the future but instead, a book to find glory and peace in. Maybe the book of Revelation is stuffed full of things that were only important for those living in that period. Maybe it's full of current events and soon-coming events specifically for a time period that affected those it was written for. Maybe we have been redeemed from almost everything written in Revelation.

Let's look into it.

John wrote the book of Revelation while imprisoned on the Isle of Patmos. Some biblical scholars believe that John used symbolic, apocalyptic, or prophetic language in an attempt to confuse his captors. It is believed that John knew that the Romans wouldn't understand what he was talking about but that all the Isrealites would completely understand the language in which he spoke. That argument makes some logical sense to me and has some validity if you consider the viewpoint that John was imprisoned by the Romans and the book of Revelation is talking about the end of the Roman Empire and what Rome is going to do to the Children of Israel and their beloved Holy Temple. Is it possible that the book of Revelation is John's Olivet Discourse?

The Olivet Discourse is the name given to the orderly and extended teaching given by Jesus Christ on the Mount of Olives. His subject is the end times. This discourse is recorded in Matthew 24:1 – 25:46. Parallel passages are found in Mark 13:1-37 and Luke 21:5-36. The record in Matthew is the most extensive until we consider the book of Revelation. It is important to recognize that Jesus' teaching in this discourse is about Israel and not the Church. Christ was speaking of God's future program for Israel. Other passages to consider when studying the Olivet Discourse are Daniel 9:24-27 and Revelation 6:1–19:21. If you notice that all the other gospels have Jesus giving his Olivet Discourse where he's talking about the End Times, the Last Days, or the destruction of the temple, etc… Notice that the Gospel of John doesn't have an Olivet Discourse from Christ on the mount of Olives. Is it possible that John did his version of the Olivet Discourse in the book of Revelation? At the beginning of the book of Revelation, the writer John says, "This is the Revelation of Jesus Christ." That sounds like good news to me. But because we have viewed it as a horrible future for ourselves, is it possible that it has blinded us from the good news of this wonderful book? Maybe we are missing the good news of the Revelation of Jesus Christ, whom we Christians claim to follow. Think about it. The story of Jesus is the gospel of peace. So is it possible that the book of Revelation is the revealing, the exposing, and the uncovering of the gospel of peace? If it is, then shouldn't we find peace and joy in the gospel of peace or the book of Revelation? Just something to think about. The book of Revelation says, "These things will happen soon," repeatedly. It mentions the End of the World but we've already clarified that it was a mistranslation. It literally means the end of an age or era or more specifically the end of the Old Covenant. The Greek word for Revelation is Apocalypsis or in our English translation Apocalypse but it doesn't mean catastrophe like our modern readers or Hollywood has made it out to seem. Apocalypsis simply means to reveal or uncover what has been hidden or unseen. Could the book of Revelation simply be the unveiling or uncovering of the good news of Jesus Christ? Is it possible that most of the End Times, end of the era, and destruction of the temple talk in the book of Revelation, the Gospels, Peter, and the Old Testament is talking about 70 AD? According to historical facts, that is when the temple was destroyed, when Jerusalem was destroyed, and when everything Jesus said would happen, actually happened in history. There are historical documents that can verify the fulfillment of the prophecies that Jesus talked about. Maybe because 70 AD is not written in the Bible we choose to not want to look at it as true. Religion can blind us to ignore anything outside of the Bible. Is it possible that all of that was fulfilled in 70 AD, within a generation, just like Jesus said? The best argument I've heard against the idea of the Book of Revelation being fulfilled in 70 AD, is the argument that the book of Revelation was written after 70 AD. There are many different debates about that and different ways to prove that it's false. But the one that stands out the most to me is literally in scripture. John writes of things that were currently happening, like who the current Caesar was at the time of his writings. We talk in more detail about this in the Mark of the Beast chapter. John talks about who the current Caesar is, and who the Caesars were before that, he talks about the next

Caesar to come afterward and it's all historically accurate and it happened within the time frame of his writing of the book of Revelation. John also mentions in Revelation that Israel still being a nation and will be destroyed in the near future. If the book of Revelation was written after 70 AD how could he still refer to Israel as a nation and why would he talk about the nation's soon-coming destruction if It had already been destroyed? He wouldn't. Because the destruction of 70 AD is a historical fact and actually happened in history, why would John write like he did if it was after 70 AD? Would he be talking to his people about something that already happened and he would be talking about it like it never did happen? That doesn't even make logical sense. So obviously he wrote it before 70 AD. Most bible scholars believe the book of Revelation was written somewhere between 64 AD and 68 AD, which is well within a decade of the destruction of the temple and the end of the era that the Bible talks about. Surely John was present and heard Jesus give the Olivet Discourse just like the other synoptic writers of the gospels yet he didn't include that long prophecy in his gospel. Then many years later while imprisoned on the Isle of Patmos,

Jesus visits him with a much more detailed and expressive view of that same Olivet

Discourse. It was a more detailed and dramatic version. Maybe one of the main reasons John was finally writing his version of Olivet Discourse, was because Jesus wanted to give His Church a Comforting update within the last decade of its coming fulfillment. History and Scripture confirm that from AD 30 to AD 70, the church suffered terrible persecution at the hands of the Jewish temple leaders and the Romans. This abuse was greatly intensified in AD 64 through AD 68 under Nero. Nero made it his goal to annihilate Christianity during this very difficult time. The church needed encouragement and comfort from Jesus. They needed reassurance that He would be coming back soon. That is just what the Book of Revelation gave them. Throughout Revelation, God tells his followers to be patient, because his justice, wrath, and vengeance will be there to save them soon. In Dr. Lynn Hiles's book titled, "Revelation of Jesus Christ," He says, "The book of Revelation is not about dreadful Beasts and scary monsters. It's an ongoing Revelation of Jesus Christ and God's redemptive plan." He states "The more you understand the book of Revelation, the more you will be disarmed of the fears, intimidations, rhetoric, the floods of misinformation flowing from the dragon's mouth." Here is a powerful fact to consider. The book of Revelation is the only book in the Bible that declares blessings on the reading and understanding of it. If you want more detailed studies and breakdowns of the book of Revelation, I encourage you to check out Dr. Lynn Hiles and Dr. Jonathan Welton. They both have books and YouTube videos you can look up about the Book of Revelation, the Rapture, etc... I just want to give a summary or maybe an alternative look to remove the fear and dread of the Book of Revelation so we can see Jesus Christ and His Good News in every verse.

CHAPTER SIXTEEN
THE GREAT TRIBULATION

Is it possible that The Great Tribulation ideology, representing Hell on Earth for seven years, is completely taken out of scriptural context? The great tribulation period has haunted and created terror in the hearts and minds of Christians for generations. The main passage used to create this fear was spoken by Jesus in Matthew chapter 24. It mentions earthquakes, pains, plagues, famines, false teachers, and sufferings, just to name a few. As I've mentioned before in other chapters in this book, you can research to confirm this information for yourself by checking church history. The fact is, that all of the First-Century Christians, all of the church fathers up until the 1800s, believed that all that Jesus spoke about in Matthew 24 was in the past. They believed it all happened in AD 70 and that the event fulfilled all of Jesus's prophecies. It wasn't until the 1800s, when false doctrine was intentionally spread abroad for political and religious reasons, that it became broadly a different view of the End Times and of what Jesus said in Matthew 24. Research it for yourself. Allow me to expose you to a little more evidence or proof that Matthew 24 was completely fulfilled in the great Jewish Revolt or Siege of Jerusalem in 70 AD and that all the church fathers previous to the 1800s knew this as well. Eusebius of Caesarea also known as Eusebius Pamphilus was a Greek Syro-Palestinian Historian of Christianity. He is known as the "Father of church history." He was the first to write a "comprehensive" history of the early church. The historian Eusebius speaking of Matthew 24 said, "All of this occurred in the second year of the reign of Roman Emperor Vespasian in AD 70." It can't get any more clear than that in my opinion. Dr. Jonathan Welton's writings led me to a great book on the historical account of Matthew 24 and its fulfillment in 70 AD with the destruction of Jerusalem. The event was written in graphic detail by the author George Peter Holford in 1805. His writings are extremely graphic and disturbing honestly. But it confirms everything Jesus had prophesied would come to pass in the last days or the end of the world. You can read a more updated version or easier-to-read version in Dr. Jonathan Welton's book, "Raptureless." The first time I read it, I had to stop reading it for a while, it was overwhelming to me and heart-wrenching. It talked about people starving in Jerusalem to the point of eating their children, etc... It goes on and on describing horrors that actually happened in Jerusalem. That was truly the great tribulation that Jesus had spoken of. Dr. Welton said, "If you search the history of the world you will not find one account of such unnatural barbarism in any other nation, in any other siege, in the history of the world as was recorded about the things that happened in the siege of Jerusalem in 70 AD!" The Jewish historian Josephus said, "If it had not been for the fact that so many credible witnesses saw these things that happened in Jerusalem, he would not have written them or recorded them because people wouldn't have believed his writings because they were such shocking violations of nature." Wow! That sounds like a great tribulation to me. I'd like to draw your attention to the fact that most biblical scholars believe that the book of Revelation is parallel to Matthew 24. So if Matthew 24 is in the past and happened already is it possible that the things written in the book

Revelation already happened as well? In scripture Jesus is recorded as saying, "There will be great tribulation." Then just a few verses later He says, "All of these things will happen before this generation standing before him passes." Is it possible that there is no future great tribulation? Sure tough times may come. This past pandemic we experienced was tough on a lot of people but it is still on no level to be considered in comparison to the level of a seven-year great tribulation period, like the one tribulation period that was fulfilled in a great Jewish revolt in 70 AD. I pray this eases your mind and gives you peace.

CHAPTER SEVENTEEN
THESE LAST AND EVIL DAYS

I have heard people say, all my life, that "We are living in the last and evil days!" They would follow that up with something like, "Just look around at all the horrible things happening all over the world today." "Jesus is surely soon to return to save us from this horrible day and age we're living in." But I wonder, is it possible that many of us simply have a pessimistic attitude, and because we're looking for those types of terrible things to occur, we manifest those terrible realities? It is all we seem to see because we are looking for those horrible things. Like the scripture says, "Seek and ye shall find." Pause and think about that for a moment. Because of misunderstanding scripture in context, could we be conditioned only to see negative things, to only look for negative realities, to expect doom and gloom? Could we possess a "Negativity Bias"?

Consider these easy examples. I could give so many more but these seven will suffice.

1. It is a fact that for the majority of our existence on the planet, it has been legal to beat your wife. This was true in almost every community, in every country. But now in "these last and evil days" if you beat your wife or your girlfriend and even if she is too scared to press charges, it wouldn't even matter. The law enforcement agency will decide to take the case upon themselves and defend your wife or girlfriend anyway, even if she is too afraid to defend herself in court. Now again that whole process does still have its flaws but man oh man, it's way better than it was just 10 years ago.

2. In these "last and evil days" The extreme poverty rate has drastically dropped in America as well as the entire planet.

3. Not too long ago in America. A black mother's only recourse if her young son or daughter was beaten or brutally raped by a white man was to hold that child, rock them and cry with them. Because there was absolutely nothing she could do about it. There was nothing the child's

father could do about it. It was legal; they were only property, and the master could do whatever they wanted to do to you or your children. Even many decades after slavery was abolished, horrible atrosities could be done to black people without repercusions. But in these "last and evil days" nothing like that even exists. As I write this chapter today we have the first female vice president in American history as well as the first black vice president in American history, who is currently running for the first Black Female President of the United States and we have recently had two terms of the first black President of the United States. Racial issues still exist but to imagine that they are even close to as bad as they used to be is unconscionable. A deceitful viewpoint has arisen due to all the camera phones that people have now, along with the cameras inside police cars as well as on police officers' uniforms. Because of all this video evidence lately, we tend to think that police brutality is at an all-time high but the actual fact is that levels of police brutality is many times better than it was just 20 years ago. Back in the 1970's, Detroit's first black mayor Coleman A. Young said what is happening is that the press and the news people are taking the total number of murders and killings in Detroit and just bunching them all together and because of that Detroit is considered the murder capital. He said that what they are neglecting to mention is how a great deal of those murders are the white police in the City of Detroit killing its black citizens. The honest truth is that the police are doing much better than they used to be and that's a fact that is documented.

4. In the 1990s when my children were being born. Out of every thousand children born, 90 of them would die before the age of five but today in these "last and evil days" (I know I'm being sarcastic) the number is less than 20 children, out of every thousand. Wow! That's awesome!

5. Just as recently as 2007, over 40 teenage girls out of every thousand got pregnant but today it's under 15 girls for every thousand. A true "sign of the times", not so bad huh?

6. In 1955 over 45 percent of the population in America smoked that is nearly half of everybody in America but today that percentage is under 15.

7. Death by homicide or assault has decreased all over the world. Just in America, our murder rate has decreased by almost double what it was in the 1980s.

You can research all this stuff for yourselves and there are many many more positive statistics I could have gotten into. I just listed the top seven that grabbed me. But if you're looking for negativity, you'll find it. If you are looking for positivity, you will find it. "Seek and you shall find." What are you looking for? What are you focusing on?

In David Hawkins book, "Letting go", in a chapter called "Owning the Shadow". He references Swiss psychiatrist and psychotherapist

Dr. Carl Jung who is the Founding Father of Analytical Psychology. Hawkins quotes Dr. Jung stating that buried inside of each of us is a collective unconscious which he calles the "Shadow" and in each of our shadows lies everything we least like about ourselves and we would rather ignore it as opposed to dealing with it. Carl Jung said, "The average human would much rather project his/her shadow onto the world and condemn it and see it as evil, thinking that his or her problem is to battle with evil in the world but in actuality the problem is merely to acknowledge the presence of such thoughts and impulses in ourselves."

Could the truth be that we see negative stuff in the world, but it's really a reflection of what's on the inside of us. An example from my own life, I was dating a girl who continually accused me of being unfaithful to her although I was not nor did I give a reason to suspect I was. Come to find out later in our relationship that she was unfaithful. So her guilt made her always think, I had be unfaithful too. In the past maybe we see a Pastor or Politician who seems to be extremely against homosexuals to the point of being abusive with attacks then after some time passes, we discover they'd be the main ones who's sleeping with boys or having gay sex. Instead of dealing with thier own shadow they project that out onto the world. You meet people who hate liars and spend time with them and discover that they lie often to themselves as well as to others. But they ignore their own shadow or darkness and project it onto the world outside of themselves. Maybe we are doing the same thing when we judge the world as getting worse, especially when almost every metric shows the world is getting better.

What are you thinking about? Whatever it is, positive or negative then yes you will see that. If you're expecting bad times or evil days then you will bring those things to you. They will surround you. You will always be around them but you have control over that. You can change that and I hope this book helps you do just that.

The Gospel is supposed to be good news. Wouldn't it be really good news to know that the horrible day of judgment that Jesus talked about had already passed? Would it be good news to know that you and your children could have a bright and hopeful future? We tend to read the Bible like it was written to us. But is it possible that it was written for us as opposed to being written to us? Think about it. I could be wrong. I simply want to present you with an alternative viewpoint, a viewpoint that I believe

leads to freedom, love, and peace. More in line with the good news that Jesus brought to us. Maybe the good news is spreading and making the world a better place. We just have to open our eyes, take off the veil of misinformation, and mistranslated scriptures that blind us from seeing the truth. So we can stop missing all the wonderful things that the good news has brought into the world. Maybe the world has changed and transformed into a better place, a safer place. Again the world still has problems but I believe the gospel, the good news, and the love of God is working and purifying.

I believe the love of God is spreading, transforming, and changing us and the world. Or maybe God and Jesus are failures? Not at all! One last thing I'd like to mention is that if you search church history, you'll find out that the

First Century believers believed that the gospel was spreading all over the planet and the world was changing for the better. They believed that the Last and Evil Days that Jesus spoke of had already passed and had happened within a generation just as he had spoken. They believed that everything was turning out for the good and getting better. They saw In their lifetimes the Romans who were their major persecutors become Christians. Things were changing for the better. Let it marinate, pray about it, and decide for yourself.

CHAPTER EIGHTEEN
THE THIEF IN THE NIGHT

The idea of destruction coming as a thief in the night used to frighten me. But maybe we have an incorrect understanding of this event. Let's look into it. Revelation chapter 16, verse 15 says, "Behold I come as a thief, blessed is he that watcheth and keepeth his garments lest he walk naked and they see his shame." Matthew chapter 24 verse 43 says, "If the goodman of the house had known in what hour the thief would come he would have watched and would not have allowed his house to be broken up." 2nd Peter 3 and 10 says, "The day of the Lord will come as a thief in the night, the Heavens shall pass away with a great noise and the elements shall melt with the fervent heat, the earth and all the works therein shall be burned up." Now honestly, all of these verses I just quoted have been explained in other chapters in this book. We dealt with the Heavens and the earth's passing away or being destroyed. We dealt with the elements melting, etc.. but all the scriptures I just quoted are all referring to events that were said in scripture to shortly come to pass. Or it said that they would happen soon that they were at hand or that they would happen before the generation standing in front of Jesus.

We discovered that history confirms that they were all fulfilled within a generation just like Jesus said in the siege of Jerusalem in 70 AD. It all went down just as Jesus and other scriptures had prophesied. In First Thessalonians chapter 5, verses 2 through 4, Paul said, "The day of the Lord will come like a thief in the night." Then Paul says, "But you brethren are not in darkness, so that day won't surprise you, like a thief in the night." Remember that according to Jewish historians Josephus and Eusebius, both were quoted as saying that not one follower of Jesus is recorded as dying in the siege of AD 70. Because they all saw the signs of the times and they fled to the mountains just like Jesus told them to do. The thief in the night didn't catch those who listened to Jesus's instructions. Maybe we shouldn't be worried about any kind of thief of the night because he has already come and gone. That warning was for those living in that time over 2000 years ago. I hope this brings you some peace and some joy.

CHAPTER NINETEEN
ARMAGEDDON

The word Armageddon brings about both fascination and extreme fear in Christians and non-Christians alike. Even in Hollywood, Armageddon has been the subject of countless movies, television shows, and documentaries. Just adding the insertion of the word in casual conversation indicates something catastrophic, or disastrous in some manner. Statements like, "When she gets angry, it's like *Armageddon*," or "The damage left behind from the earthquake is like *Armageddon*," are just some of the ways that the word has been used to lend its negative connotations. I'm kinda excited to expose the truth of this word that used to terrify me. We find our first references to the word in the Old Testament, however, in another form. There it is referred to as "Megiddo" – the valley of Megiddo to be exact. It is here that the great king Josiah, who reigned in Judah from the age of eight, would meet his demise after thirty-one years. In Second Chronicles chapter 35, verses 22 through 24, it reads, "Nevertheless Josiah would not turn his face from him, but disguised himself, that he might fight with him, and hearkened not unto the words of Necho from the mouth of God, and came to fight in the valley of Megiddo. And the archers shot at King Josiah, and the king said to his servants, 'Have me away; for I am sore wounded.' His servants, therefore took him out of that chariot and put him in the second chariot that he had, and they brought him to Jerusalem, and he died, and was buried in one of the sepulchers of his fathers. And all Judah and Jerusalem mourned for Josiah." This is not talking about a futuristic event. But let's look a little deeper while using some historical facts to shed some light on the Great War of Armageddon. In Revelation chapter 16 the reader will see that the seven plagues of Revelation 16 are a very accurate description of several notable events throughout the Jewish War. The pouring out of the seven bowls of Revelation 16 is a reflection of the pouring out of drink offerings during Pentecost. During Pentecost in A.D. 66, Josephus and Tacitus record what appears to be the departure from the Temple of the seven angels with the seven bowls. Immediately thereafter, the Jewish War began. During this war, the seas and rivers turned red with blood as predicted in the second and third bowls. A multitude of miraculous signs were witnessed in A.D. 69, one year before the climactic siege of Jerusalem in fulfillment of Revelation 16:14: "They are spirits of demons performing miraculous signs, and they go out to the kings of the whole world, to gather them for the battle . . . ." Amidst these miraculous signs, the kings of the east, Sohaemus and Antiochus, crossed the Euphrates to meet the other Roman forces near Mt. Megiddo (Armageddon) as indicated in Revelation 16:12 and 16. During this time a great thunderstorm and earthquake simultaneously rocked Jerusalem while both Rome and Jerusalem were divided by separate and concurrent three-way civil wars as predicted in the seventh bowl in Revelation 16:18-19: "Then there came flashes of lightning, rumblings, alot of thunder and a severe earthquake. The great city split into three parts." When the Romans arrived in Jerusalem in A.D. 70, Roman catapults hurled boulders into the city. These stones were white and weighed about one hundred pounds as predicted in Revelation 16: 21: "From the sky huge hailstones of about a hundred pounds each fell upon men." All that you've just read may seem unbelievable. However, most information is taken from unbiased historical records and all information is easily verifiable.

CHAPTER TWENTY
FINAL THOUGHTS

I've been around for over half a century. I remember in the 70s, they were talking about, these are last days the world is about to end. I remember the 80s, these are last days the world is about to end. Look at all that's happening in the world. The mark of the beast, the 666 is any day now, Ronald Reagan is the Antichrist. The 90s, the 2000s but even more so is decades before I was even born, people were still thinking, These are the last days. Bob Marley thought he was living in the last days. I mean, just go on and on again. I remember hearing a joke that some might find offensive but that I could't help but to laugh at, it went: "Jesus is black, you know how I know?" How do you know? "Because he been saying he gonna come back for over 2000 years, and He still ain't showed up yet, He late." Hilarious to me!!

Allow me to admit that I never claim to be the most learned in the area of bible prophecy. I usually avoided it for the majority of my life because it was frightening and somewhat confusing but over the years of growing in my relationship with God I began to see many things I believed about scripture as being based more upon things I was taught from the pulpit as opposed to being accurate in scripture. This has caused me to go back into scripture and study them without attaching the decades of influential ministers and teachers leading my viewpoints. I don't believe any of them were trying to teach me in error. They have been misled themselves and believe a lot of things that were taught to them just like I have for many years myself. This book is not an exhaustive teaching on these subjects, only another idea or viewpoint for you to ponder and decide for yourself. I encourage you to do your research and study to satisfy your mind and heart. Even if I have strong views about anything in this book or life, I try my best to not tell you what to believe. I used to do that and even did it to my children while raising them in Christianity but I was so wrong about so many things and maybe I'm wrong about the things in this book. These views or revelations of scripture have freed me and brought me joy and peace and my only prayer is that they do the same for you. I will give some other books and articles for you to read if you are interested. Thank you for reading this book. If it is a blessing to you, please share it and leave a review on whatever platform you purchased this book.

FOR DEEPER STUDY, CHECK OUT:

1. Milton S. Terry, Biblical Apocalyptics: A Study of the Most Notable Revelations of God and of Christ, (Grand Rapids: Baker Book House, 1988), 21-22.

2. David Chilton, The Great Tribulation, (Fort Worth, TX: Dominion Press, 1987), 124.

3. Tacitus The Histories 5.13.

4. Josephus The Wars of the Jews 6.5.3.

5. George Holford, The Destruction of Jerusalem, (Frankford, PA: First Rate Publishers, 1812), 15.

6. "Raptureless" by Dr. Jonathan Welton

7. "Revelation of Jesus Christ" by Dr. Lynn Hiles

8. Ibid., 6.9.3.

9. Arthur M. Ogden, The Avenging of the Apostles and Prophets: Commentary on Revelation, (Pinson, AL: Ogden Publications, 2006), 308-310.

10. Josephus The Wars of the Jews 2.13.6.

www.ingramcontent.com/pod-product-compliance
Lightning Source LLC
Chambersburg PA
CBHW060520030426
42337CB00015B/1955